HOW TO START A CLOTHING LINE

POWERFUL GUIDELINES FOR BUILDING A FASHION LABEL FROM SCRATCH

By

MAXWELL ROTHERAY

Copyright © Maxwell Rotheray – All rights reserved.

No part of this publication shall be reproduced, duplicated or transmitted in any way or by any means, digital or otherwise, including photocopying, scanning, uploading, recording and translating or by any information storage or retrieval system, without the written consent of the author.

Table of Contents

Introduction 5

How to Prepare for Success 8

Making The Right Connections 13

Building A Winning Team 21

    Steps to Hiring Great Staff Team 21

Cost of Starting a Clothing Line Business 26

Finding The Right Location 33

Business Plan for Successful Clothing Line 38

How to Raise Money 43

Licensing Your Clothing Line 46

Branding Your Clothing Line 50

Preparing for A Successful Opening Day 54

How to Market Your Business for Long-Term Success 59

Steps to Scale Up in The Shortest Time Possible 64

Mistakes to avoid 68

Laws/Rules to Abide by to Avoid Legal Complications 73

Cloth Sewing Guidelines to Assure the Safety of Your Workers and Customers 77

How to Use Technology to Boost the Business 82

Artificial intelligence (AI) 85

    Internet of Things (IOT) 85

    Rapid Data Analysis for Quick Adaptation ... 86

    Mobile Commerce 86

Other Books by the Same Author 88

Introduction

It is possible you've been sketching a piece of clothing since your childhood, and have been making your design for decades; in fact, you may have already sold out thousands of custom vests you have put together in your country home. Or maybe you're just obsessed with styles and want to cut a piece of the billion-dollar clothing market.

Having an innate ability is essential and even the passion to be in the clothing industry is also important. But regardless of your motivation, knowing how to start a clothing line is very different from just wanting to go into a clothing line business. Designers are not only born; they are made as well. So having the drive and entrepreneurial acumen, you must also understand the steps through which you will have to walk to your clothing label.

By the way, the term "clothing line" refers to the process of designing and making what can be called your clothing, while exercising the power of controlling and directing the production process from beginning to the end. This means that you are in charge of the clothing line from start to finish.

With the intense competition out there, the complexities of the trade, and also the intimidation that overcloud the fashion industry, you must be concerned that as a newbie entrepreneur with little or no experience; you will not find your feet in the fashion industry. Not at all, in the fashion world, it is a different ball game. Fashion millionaires made it because of their passion and due diligence and not because of their specialized education and training. It is not a question of certification and paper qualification, but a question of mastering the trade and gaining confidence and industrial experience; standing shoulder to shoulder with big industry players without feeling intimidated. Devote your time and energy into putting together your clothing line, and you are on your way to creating a world-class clothing label.

How to Prepare for Success

If you have decided to become an entrepreneur and start your clothing line, the road no doubt is going to be exciting but challenging so be prepared for the rough path ahead. Some of the preparation you need to do may include the following:

Acquire the necessary skills: it is essential to have some training or education in design, textiles, garment creation, and sewing besides having creative ideas and a passion for cutting and sewing

Though you can place orders and have your clothes produced in a factory in mass, it is preferable if you can draw and produce concepts for the factory to follow in the production. When you eventually create a design, you will be able to test run it before the full-scale production so that your loss will be minimal if the public doesn't approve of it.

Joining classes in textiles, design, and business marketing should be of immense benefit to you and the clothing industry. Even a university education will help you expand your knowledge fast and give you an edge over your competitors. It will also provide access to feedback from colleagues and professionals, but eventually, having been able to develop creative ideas and translating them into good designs is personal – it is about you, your style, and your ability.

Do you feel having a clothing line suits you?

You must take stock of yourself and be able to decide if you are really suited to having your clothing line. Only you should determine if you have a strong design ethic, artistic know-how, and the passion for crafting your own clothing line.

Passion counts in the clothing industry:

It is possible to go into any business passionless and excel in your line of trade. Many entrepreneurs have succeeded in their chosen trade without being passionate about it. What is required mainly is due diligence, and profit will keep on flowing in. This may not likely happen in the clothing business. You must have a real passion for your brand or business model before being successful since you simply cannot enjoy your work that fails to translate into real success

You must be who you are:

One thing you shouldn't try to do is copy others in the fashion industry; your brand's personality is everything you are. This means that if you are what you think you are – creative, passionate, and original, then put it into action by coming up with a clothing line.

What your brand should be?

Branding your clothing line is very important because in this kind of business if you don't have a strong brand identity, you are likely to be ignored. Look around and try to discover how different brands came about. You will see that many available brands have a great beginning, even those that were started just to make more money.

Branding is not about passion, fashion out what you want to add to what already exists: ego, quality, better alternatives, expanded sizes, or even something completely new fashion, it is very essential to give you a base for your brand which will also serve you in the future as a guide.

It is no good business when fashioning out what you consider to be the brand you are prying into competitors' brands, no, not at all. You must take a cue from your experiences and who you are as a base. You must be able to convince the consumers that you are clever and have genuinely come up with something unique and appealing.

What do you plan to be your goal?

It doesn't matter what you consider as your goal, big or small, you must be more realistic when choosing your goal. Your goal might be related to profit, the level of public awareness your brand will generate, or the joy that your dream of having a clothing label has come true. Whatever is your dream goal, it must be realistic, achievable, and specific. Your clothing label can be out there as a side passion to generate income; the important thing is to know exactly what you want.

What about your marketing tricks?

The next question is how will you market your brand? It doesn't make sense to turn out designer clothes without making adequate arrangements on how to dispose of them. Though nowadays there are many outlets available, you must choose the ones that will play the tricks and get your wares out of your warehouse.

All these points listed are no doubt long but they are a reminder of what you are likely to face shortly if you go into the clothing business. Therefore, as you embark on the journey to launching your clothing line, you will have to do a proper investigation into the clothing industry and market, competitive activities, how consumers embrace the fashion world, and the likely trends in the future.

Making The Right Connections

Making the right connections may be achieved simply by getting seriously involved in projects of your community and beyond. Your kind of business is the one that needs many people to be successful. You have to know many people right from the staff of the local boutique which sells fashion clothes and accessories to people who patronize big retail stores. You will have boundless opportunities speaking with wonderful folks in different areas of endeavor and doing great things in your community. It also makes business sense focusing on connecting with competitors in the industry and knowing the big industry players. But first things first, look for ways to mingle with your local people and make contributions to your local community to get you recognized. There are so many ways you can connect with them and quickly get noticed:

Promote your local community distinct cause:

You can search for the stuff your community is made of and what makes them proud. Find it and promote it. Use it as if it is part of your business and have the sticker on your signage, and believe it or not, your local community will be excited to see it. Other things that make the community proud you can promote may include the following:

• Promote your City's celebrated anniversary or founder's day and get it printed on your merchandise.

• Join to celebrate with your local sport's hero's when they come on top.

• Create a radio jingle, a slogan, or make a logo that is a symbol of local pride.

- Name some of your lines after local champions, memorial sites, and landmarks.

Promote Other People

You are likely to get noticed when you promote others pursuing a credible cause. When you look around you will notice special events happening in your local community, some notable people or organizations are promoting it. Local businessmen and women like you are sponsoring charitable cause and different groups of people taking up great challenges to raise funds for a heart foundation or a fashion house donating items of clothing to a motherless baby's home. Find a way to promote those people; I can assure you that it will go a long way to connect you to your community.

Here are some of the intelligent ways to promote other people and businesses in your area:

Share human interest stories from local news outlets about inspirational people and businesses.

Use your Facebook page and Twitter to share some people and businesses especially in the fashion industry that enjoy a tremendous measure of success in your neighborhood, and congratulate them.

Donate clothes to orphanage homes.

Pledge to provide clothes for a local school uniform or provide the uniform at giveaway prices.

Head-Up a Cause

If supporting others doesn't work for you, you can begin your own cause for the benefit of your community. It could be a campaign against oppression, police brutality, extrajudicial killings, or lack of government assistance in your area. Your cause is an indication of goodwill and your contribution to the cause of the community and the people will be happy to have you as fighting for their cause and this will go a long way to promote you and your business.

You can also help to promote any of the following causes:

Survivors of natural disasters in your area.

Elderly peoples' home in your community

Students who are victims of the COVID 19 lockdown who can benefit from online coaching

Donate for a just cause

If you are not ready to organize something on your own, then find out if there is someone else in your area doing a similar thing, you can lend your moral support as well as donating clothes, money, or your time, as the case may be.

Find out in your area whether there are charitable organizations in dire need of a financial assistant or other events where the money is urgently needed, donate generously but don't forget to get such donations publicized.

Sponsor physically challenged peoples' sporting event

Supporting sporting events for the physically challenged people is one of the ways to get involved in community affairs. This option makes you satisfied all the way through but more importantly, it makes you an integral part of the community.

Local Advertising

If you are scouting for a cheap way to get noticed and generate publicity, and indeed getting your brand name and logo recognized within your neighborhood, instead of sponsoring kids' sporting events or making charitable donations, you can advertise your brand of clothing line business in the local newspaper and radio. You can also have your posters signage around the town particularly within the densely populated areas.

Apart from posters, you can put up a billboard at strategic places such as crossroads and subway busy roads. You will also use signage close to the area people do park their cars most of the time.

Participate in Events

Participate in events that take place in and around your community particularly, fashion-related events. Other events such as concerts, sports or anniversaries—you should also attend because it is one of the ways to get you noticed. If you drive, get your car painted with your business color and logo, and if possible park at a place your car will be visible.

If there is an opportunity for a fashion show, please do attend because it is an opportunity to socialize with other label owners and captains of the big retail outlets. Feel free to share pleasantries with the people and it is an opportunity to learn so much about the clothing trade and instil confidence in you as you journey to greatness. Always budget for the amount you invest in a charitable cause so that you don't deeply upset your budget in the name of supporting a charitable cause.

Some people would like to see fashion designers at events such as;

Swimwear exhibition

Summertime fashion shows

Footwear exhibition

Made in China clothes shows

Community art fairs

Weekly fashion shows

Trade shows

Building A Winning Team

All the staff you take on board should all have one technical knowledge or the other to be productive. Hiring the right technical staff is crucial to the proper take-off and smooth running of the clothing label. Even if you are operating on a small scale you certainly need an assistant from day one and this number will increase over time.

At the start-up period, you may be able to work with volunteer close friends, family members, or a partner, if you are operating at an extremely low budget, but as time progresses and your clothing business is making progress, some part-time or full-time employees will need to be hired. Moreover, when it comes to the business of clothing labels, you'll need to go the extra mile of hiring the right team members.

Steps to Hiring Great Staff Team

Due to the level of staff turnover in the fashion world, hiring employees is indeed one of the most difficult tasks for any fashion designer to handle.

Vendors often work hard to screen out the unqualified candidates at the beginning of the employment process. They often work hard because they are passionate about bringing into the market today the fashion of tomorrow.

Label owners who are unable to make good hiring decisions usually need to struggle when trying to hire competent staff. Others who are experienced in good hiring practices don't struggle. The good news is that today we'll provide you with five steps to help you out in the hiring process.

Determine your employee needs

It would seem very like counseling, but defining your employee needs should be the first approach: here we are referring to the job specification and the employee profile.

• Physical requirements: How to fit as the potential employee in terms of activities such as being creative, working under pressure, standing or sitting for too long, holding objects, and interacting with colleagues. Choose employees based on the actual requirements of the specific job – job specification.

•   Experience: This includes how long the potential employee has worked in the clothing industry, together with basic education, since there is the need to write details of a potential customer. However, be wary of the stuff the individual is made up of and the result expected and not necessarily the work history.

•   Behavior: This includes work code, the ability to be creative and apply due diligence, and be ready to interact with other employees and members of the public. It is possible to learn skills while on the job but not behavior.

• Intelligence: Basic intelligence is necessary to work in the fashion house such as the ability to cut and sew, use the right button, make buttonholes at the right position, pack each shirt in the right box, and indeed, need not be reminded of his/her tasks every time, so be smart and hire the smart people.

• Know what you have to offer: As a clothing label company, you must be yourself; cut your coat according to your cloth and don't try to compete with the big players in the industry at least at the start-up stage. Offering your employees competitive rates is important but be smart not to take more than you can chew. The big players can offer higher rates because their foundation is solid and they are generating the money.

Focus on those that can do the job. Decide on exactly what you are looking for, so you can quickly remove the chaff from the real thing. This translates to no favoritism for friends and family members but on those fit and proper people to do the job. The people you recruit must focus not on a higher compensation plan but your mission.

It is possible that competent people can attract big money, but it is also possible that big money by itself does not attract the right candidates. So focus on recruiting and developing smart employees because they are the engine of your clothing label productivity and growth.

Seek for different opinions

Be open-minded and allow everyone to be heard including participants in the hiring process because they are likely to offer you invaluable insight and prevent you from making avoidable mistakes. Something you missed may be captured by others. Though the decision about who to recruit lies with you, others may make valuable contributions in the recruiting process.

Conduct background checks on your potential employees.

Don't take anything for granted when recruiting, always conduct thorough background checks on the potential staff to reduce the incidence of hiring bad eggs. Dishonest employees can wreck your clothing business. The Small Business

Administration has emphatically said that theft accounts are responsible for about 30 percent of all business failures in the US. A high percentage isn't it. So being smart in this case is a sure way to make progress and succeed in your clothing label business.

Cost of Starting a Clothing Line Business

The cost of starting a clothing line depends on the scale you would like to operate. Some costs are fixed and remain fixed for a long time but others are recurrent. The actual cost of starting a clothing line can't be determined with every amount of certainty until some of the equipment and tools are paid for. What we are going to do in this article is to give you details of those items you need to pay for to start your business as well as costs that can influence the startup capital.

The following are the areas of cost that determines how much money you are going to spend on start-up.

Manufacturing costs

It is important to have a marketing plan prepared. The cost of producing the dresses yourself will require that you procure different types of sewing machines and other tools, but if you are outsourcing the production, it also depends on the country you are in. For instance, if you are in the US and producing just 100 pieces of each dress, it may cost you an average of $23 per piece of dress and it is likely to cost you even lower if instead of 100 pieces, it is 1,000 pieces. But for a similar job to be done in China, it may cost you as low as $14 and is likely to be lower if you increase the quantity to 1,000 pieces.

To arrive at the manufacturing costs, you may need to do some basic calculation of multiplying the number produced with the different category of dresses, and then with the cost per unit.

Product Sourcing Costs

As a newbie in the clothing label business, you might have to part with some money on sourcing for quality materials and fabrics particularly if you are going to handle the sewing yourself, but if you would be outsourcing the entire production, then you might not have to worry about this cost.

Raw material costs

For a dress that you paid $50 for production, you shouldn't expect to spend less than $30 per piece on the fabric, labels, packaging, and similar costs.

Delivery costs

This is can be looked at in two ways. In the first place, you would have to spend money on shipping your materials from the manufacturer's down to your warehouse. Occasionally, you might be lucky to get free shipping from your manufacturer. But then, you would also have to think of shipping the goods to your buyers when there is an order so as not to discourage them from patronizing your line.

Marketing costs

This is where a marketing plan plays a role. The marketing plan should provide you with information to arrive at these costs.

You should make provision for adverts funds, sales promotion like different incentives, discounts, giving out samples as well as driving traffic to your website or blog using SEO techniques—and all of these cost money. So you should be prepared to spend up to $1,200 to execute marketing and advertisement programs; although it is possible you spend lower.

Product Photography and Modelling

Clothes only appeal to people when they are worn and displayed. It is the more reason why you would hire the services of a professional photographer and models to take photos of your various designs you bill to display on your site and product catalog.

Designing Costs

Designing is an important aspect of branding, and of course, you would want your brand to stand out by the unique designs you produce. For this reason, you would need to engage the services of a professional designer who would change the look of every dress you turn out – but it is going to be at a cost.

Designer's fees vary but depend on the complexity of work done. Designers charge can range from $10 per piece to $300 but it is not uncommon for designers to charge as much as $500 to $1,000.

Website Development

You should need a website or at least a blog to display your various designs. You should expect to pay as little as $300 but as high as $2,000. If you want a lot of features integrated into your website, you should budget for it.

Warehousing and Storage

Storage is also part of the initial cost though you shouldn't expect to have huge stocks of both raw materials and finished goods all year round.

Business registration and licencing

Business registration and licensing costs are standard and you should browse the exact fee and include it as part of the costs.

Overhead costs

Overhead Costs such as rent, salaries, and wages, transportation, lighting, and telephone costs should be estimated.

Distribution Costs

When your brands are ready, you must spend money on distribution to ensure your customers get the products. Usually, distributors for your brands buy in large quantities at cheaper rates and sell to make a profit. You will be spending more money to retail the products if you choose to have your store. But you must have at least a showroom.

Insurance

Insurance is important so you must budget for it. Apart from being required by law, you need insurance to cover the risks of fire, burglary, and life.

Product Launching

To bring to the notice of your community, you must launch your line in a dignified way which may be an opportunity to sponsor an event; if possible organizing a fashion show. It is not going to consume a small budget.

Celebrity Endorsements

Celebrity endorsement is now regarded as a marketing gimmick designed to drive sales and increase revenue generation. It is a good option but the cost is always high. Here it can be as low as $1,000 and as high as $5000, for a medium-sized clothing line.

Gross total

If your home country is the US, you should begin to budget your start-up cost to be in the range of $500,000 to $1 million, it can be less or more for a small scale clothing line business.

Finding The Right Location

When it comes to choosing a location for a clothing line, you don't make the mistake of rushing to a decision, because here your location should be used as a manufacturing site as well as your outlet for revenue generation. You have to conduct thorough market research and environmental scan before coming to a decision. If need be, get a property agent who will find a good location for your clothing line. Take note of the following factors in your search:

• **Location Demographics**-: The importance of this is obvious. You must consider your niche and its location. Then you look for a location where your potential customers are likely to be regular. For example, if you sell to women, how many of them pass through the area where you want to locate.

As a follow-up, you undertake a simple survey to be convinced that the human and vehicle traffic around the area translates to shoppers. Observe the clothing stores around the area and the human traffic in and out of the shops every day. Observe also those who are in the area for window shopping.

• **Accessibility**-: how reachable is the place you plan to site your business? Is it close or far away from the town? Is it accessible and frequently used by many people? Can I use the road if I were going shopping? What about parking your car in a safe place without getting a parking ticket or the car being towed away before you are out of the shop?

Customers look for these basic conveniences before they stop to do shopping. So in making your choice of a suitable location, you must consider all these basic conveniences.

• **Visibility**-: This is also an important factor. Apart from making the site if your business visible, you are likely to spend less on an advertisement. If you site your business where it can easily be seen, some out of curiosity would pop in someday to give your shop a trial.

• **Safety and Security**-: Security is also important to customers. You need safety too. You need to find out the security history of the place where you want to use it for your business. Some areas are chronically notorious for thefts and break-ins and such areas should be avoided as much as possible.

Prevention, they say is better than cure. So, to avoid such problems, find out how safe is the place. Get information from existing tenants. What security measures are adopted already to protect life and property in the area? Fire outbreaks can also be a problem, so find out if there are businesses nearby that are prone to fire outbreaks.

• **Competition**- Find and locate your business where there are other businesses in the same line. Competition is not a bad thing after all; instead, it draws customers if you have many clothing businesses in the area. The area becomes a business center for body wears.

•   **Affordability**-: You also have to be mindful of your budget to make sure you choose a place where you can conveniently afford without putting unnecessary pressure on your finances. Other incidental costs you must not overlook include the cost of remodeling the apartment; include utility bills, maintenance expenses, and relative taxes.

• **Zoning laws**-: You must conduct detailed research in the area of zoning laws to make sure future developments in the area are not going to affect your business. So, find out if some future constructions and expansions are likely to affect your business in the nearest future. Find out from the agency in charge of town planning before you sign a rent agreement.

• **Image**-: The image you want to create for your clothing line should match your location. So what image do you want to create for your business? For instance, you want your store to be known as an upscale boutique that sells high-class designer clothing, if that is the case, you cannot open your business in an obscure area not visited by high-class people who can afford such clothes. If you do you will probably run the risks of running out of business in the shortest space of time. Match your location with the class of clothing line you have decided to project.

• **Success of similar businesses**-: Your initial research should cover how the existing businesses in the area are faring. If they are doing well, then assuming your clothing line meets the needs of your potential customers, it is likely you are going to make a success of your clothing line.

Business Plan for Successful Clothing Line

Every business owner should create a road map that leads to where managers should be focusing their efforts to achieve the goals of the business. It is the first step to take when you decide to go into the clothing line business. The business plan may also be very useful if you want to attract investors, obtain a bank loan, and get your clothing line up and running. The following outline of your clothing line business plan should provide information that will enable you to run your clothing line and here you are:

1. An executive summary. An executive summary introduces your clothing business and provides a synopsis of your business plan. It should present information in a concise but sufficient as to what the overall plan should be like. The plans should be discussed in greater detail in subsequent aspects of the goal.

2. Company description. This section describes your clothing line business, when it started, who is behind its creation and needs that are there to be fulfilled, and what are the goals they have set out to achieve. The section should describe your passion and the niche of the market you have chosen to serve including why they should patronize your business instead of competitors'.

3. Market analysis. Here, you give details of which market segment you have chosen to satisfy their needs. Details also should be provided on where your customers are located and how they can be reached both in terms of physical distribution and advertising. This section is where you are going to demonstrate your knowledge of the clothing line and which clothing label your business will be bringing to the market at start-up.

4. Organization and management. You will have to provide sufficient information here on how you are going to organize your

business about how it is going to relate to the outside world (e.g., sole proprietor, partnership, LLC). This section also gives information concerning who are the brains behind the clothing line business, their percent shareholdings, and who will assume the mantle of leadership (CEO).

5. Service/product range. For a clothing line company, your product is mainly diverse brands of clothes you are going to sell in different outlets – online and physical stores. You will have to provide information about your wares – different markets they are meant for and what tactics you are going to deploy to attract customs. What plans do you have in the offing for identifying new needs, expanding your market, and attacking competitors?

6. Marketing and sales strategies. This is the section you provide a broad plan on how the clothing line company is going to meet the company's goals. It will show how the target market is to be selected, how the clothing line is going to be positioned in the market,

and the planning and implementation of programs (products, price, promotion, and distribution) required to achieving the profit target.

Also, there should be information on how to identify other marketing efforts to be used to generate sales such as paid ads, social media platforms, website creation, and what will give you a competitive advantage.

7. Funding proposal. This section provides detailed analysis concerning funding that is necessary at start-up as well as for the smooth running of the clothing line. Also, there will be information on how funding should be sought and from where – either in the form of bank borrowing or the use of other ways of attracting financiers or outside investors. This section should give details of how much money should be required and how it is going to be spent to run and grow the business.

8. Financial projections. As a new clothing business, there is no information about the

financial history of the business. However, with the marketing and sales strategy in place, an estimate will show a rough projection of the income and expenditure for the next six months to one year.

How to Raise Money

Finance is the backbone of every business and sourcing for funds to finance it may be the biggest challenge you are likely to face at a start-up in the clothing line business.

But not to worry so much because there are so many options you can choose from to raise money. But first prepare a comprehensive business plan which will highlight every aspect of your clothing line including the type and number of labels you will be creating, who are the buyers, what will be your sales projection, and the expected profit. You should also prepare yourself to be creditworthy both as an individual and at the business level since it is likely to be a factor when your application is being processed.

There are other options to get funding for your new clothing line business.

Here are some of the ways to launch your business with minimal funding:

- Start your business at a very low scale, if possible with your savings.

- Launch a private, black or white label and avoid launching a designer label until a later date

- Launch your business first by cutting and sewing and selling them to the local people.

- You may speak to fashion designers who are successful in running a fashion house about managing part of the clothing label.

- Seek an angel investor. These financial experts are out there looking for a new investor with which they would like to partner financially. The clothing line might just be the kind of creative endeavor that an angel investor is looking for, and you can find groups in every state.

- You may attempt to obtain a business loan especially if you already have a payment processor.

- Personal savings – use your savings

- Bank loans – approach your bankers for a medium-term loan.

- Through the US Small Business Administration

- Partnering with someone who can release his/her funds.

- Obtaining finance from a commercial finance company.

- Going through the venture-capital route.

Licensing Your Clothing Line

Clothing line businesses need multiple permits and licenses before they can legally operate in the US. Depending on your country or city, the clothing line business requirements may not be the same.

In some countries, you may be required to register your business annually, while in other countries, registering your clothing line business is performed only once.

Here are the common clothing line licenses and permits which you are likely required to obtain before you start to operate.

- Employer Identification Number

Clothing line businesses usually operate with several workers. However, for your business to operate in line with the law, you have to obtain an employer identification number (EIN).

The IRS uses your EIN to identify your business and collect the applicable taxes from you and your employees.

All business owners can obtain the employer identification number for free from their respective states by browsing the IRS website.

- Business License

Every business that operates in America should have a valid business license to operate. Floating and running your business without a business license is too risky in the US, as those who have been caught have all been severely sanctioned.

So, visit any local government office close to you to obtain a valid business license to guarantee a safe and legal operation of your clothing line business.

- Seller's Permit

Apparels are not immune from taxation so if you are into the clothing line business you need a Sellers' Permit as well as a "Certificate of Authority". With this certificate, you will be able to buy raw materials to make fabric without paying sales tax.

Also, they can collect sales tax from customers on clothing items and remit the tax to the relevant state.

- Apparel registration certificate: Many American states demand that you register your business with the state government if you manufacture items. Since you do this by cutting, sewing, assembling, and pressing fabrics, you will need the certificate even before starting your business.

- Fire Certificates

If you have a retail shop or space for manufacturing, you should obtain a permit from the fire department and be ready to comply with their guidelines for the safety of your employees and others.

Since you are likely to have your own retail space, you will need other permits like the alarm, occupational, building, worker's compensation insurance among others.

- Sign permit:

Some cities control the signs you mount outside your business, including lighting, size, location, and so on.

• Insurance: This is a legal requirement and also will likely be most expensive since it includes health, disability, general liability, and business overhead expense disability insurance.

Branding Your Clothing Line

A brand is essentially a seller's promise to deliver a specific set of features, benefits, and services consistently to the buyers. The best brands convey a warranty of quality

The process of branding your clothing line business may be the most critical and yet challenging decision you will come upon as an entrepreneur. Your brand is the relationship your customers have with your business. Creating a brand that makes a great impression on your customers and inspires loyalty is all about creating a unique brand identity that includes a well-designed logo.

A well-branded clothing line will undoubtedly catch the attention of potential customers and draw them close to you.

On the other hand, giving less attention to branding your clothing line business will set you on a course that will generate little or no sales.

Here are the steps to take if you want to brand your clothing line business.

- Know your brand

People are attracted by what they see, and only an attractive brand will draw customers to your business.

This step should aim to identify what your brand is and how it is going to generate sales for the business. If you cannot lay your hands on anything, think about the passion that drove you to set up a clothing line business. What is the unique selling proposition (USP) that you have created to generate customers? Use it to craft your brand and choose a catchy brand name.

- Design an effective logo for your brand

Remember that your logo makes the first impression for your business, so be careful to craft an impressive logo

- Build a culture around your brand

To build a culture around your brand, you must first of all identify the culture you are seeking to appeal to and enlarge.

- Concentrate on what makes you unique

This is where the passion that drove you into the clothing line comes in. Develop your unique selling proposition and use it to set yourself apart from other competitors.

- Focus on customer service

Customer service plays the role of bringing the customers back even when issues are not resolved in their favor.

- Polarize your audience

Taking a position and standing on it will set you apart from the rest of the competitors. Let your customers know where you stand within their culture and what you represent.

- Launch your brand

Make effective connections with your audience in an offline setting and use online properties to leverage those relationships.

Preparing for A Successful Opening Day

Your opening day is important in your business life and it must be taken seriously. It is so important because it is the day when all you have planned for years pays off, and it is also the first day that sets you on your way to success as a clothing line owner in the years ahead.

This is why it is essential to plan properly to make your opening day a huge success.

Below, we have put together a whole load of tips to help take you through the preparation and show you how to go about it properly on an opening day

Try to draw the crowd

It's your opening day and should work as much as possible to make it successful by drawing the attention of the public to your clothing line as much as possible. Even if they don't intend to buy the first day, you should plan to make them participate in the activities of the day or at least notice your presence/clothing line business.

While it may be difficult to attract a large crowd to your clothing line business the very first day of its existence, it is possible to achieve it using the right marketing strategy.

Some methods available you can employ to draw members of the public is through social media and giving out mouth-watering offers that are irresistible.

1.	Bear in mind that not all you have planned will be executed with precision and so be prepared to act.

While you may have done everything in the hope that they will be executed according to plan, you should also bear in mind that something might go wrong.

Now, this doesn't mean that something will go wrong, what we are saying is that you should prepare for the worst-case scenario and be ready in case something goes wrong.

You certainly do not want to be caught chasing a rat when your house is on fire. As you are close to the opening day, compile a list of some likely hiccups and look for their solutions before the launch begins proper.

2. Give your first customers a coupon for their subsequent visit

The real evidence that shows a successful opening day is convincing your first-time customers to come back again and again.

Giving your customers reasons to come back, again and again, maybe the most difficult challenge you will face after your opening day.

So, you need to apply tact and strategize to bring them back again. One of these strategies is to offer them a generous discount for their next purchase in your clothing line store.

3. Act politely as you interact with your customers

To have a successful opening day and gain your customer's confidence, you need to interact with them politely and with an open mind.

Also, you will need to use the golden opportunity to speak on a topic that is geared towards marketing your clothing line. You can do this by starting an interesting conversation while those that have ordered for clothes are being served.

If you can successfully do that, they wouldn't mind patronizing your shop in due time.

4.   Collect their contacts

In the course of your interaction with them, request for their contact information, not everything but just phone number to send them your clothing line updates.

While some will oblige to the proposal, the vast majority will be hesitant to release their contact details on their first day to new clothing line business. With the contact information in your possession, you can begin a long-term relationship with these customers by keeping them up to date and inviting them for clothing line fashion shows and other exhibitions.

How to Market Your Business for Long-Term Success

Without applying the process of marketing and sales, your business will begin to disintegrate because no meaningful sales will be generated in the face of stiff competition

The clothing line business requires adequate planning, improving on the marketing strategy, and selling your wares to the target audience.

Carrying all these out diligently will set you on the part to sustaining long-term success. The clothing line business is associated with a brand and fashion but they are different in their way.

Each business should have a marketing strategy that will generate sales and sustain it for a long time.

Here are some of the ways through which clothing line owners can market their wares and sustain sales for long-term success:

- Try to be unique

There is intense competition in the clothing line business and this could pose a threat to sustaining sufficient sales on a long-term basis.

So, to stand out among competitors and sustain long-term success for your clothing business, you must change tactics and do things differently from what others are doing.

For example, instead of coming up with the common names that clothing lines business owners have, you can craft a different and unique name that can attract the attention of people around you.

Other strategies you can execute differently from others include creating an outstanding logo and having a special branding.

- Find an online presence

The web is the perfect market space to market your clothing line business for long-term success. No matter how the things around you evolve, the need for the internet is growing and it is going to remain that way in the foreseeable future.

Millions of people all over the world browse the internet on a daily basis, seeking one information or the other.

You can get a web designer to create an interactive website for your business as well as creating social media handles that provide necessary information for your clothing line business.

An active interactive website is crucial for the sustenance of the long-term success of any business as it provides potential customers with your location address as well as your offerings.

Anyone can be using the internet casually and come across your clothing line business name and they may decide to try it out for real.

Furthermore, you can hire an SEO expert to work out something that will make your website rank high in search engines when people search for clothes.

- Advertise/Email marketing

Advertising is a known means of letting people know about your existence and what your business offers.

Different ways to advertise include the following:

Printing of flyers and getting it distributed to targeted places.

Using local newspapers and radio to advertise your wares.

While advertising depletes the budget with large sums of money, the positive effects of advertising cannot be quantified.

Email marketing is another means to promote your clothing lines and it works by getting people to sign up to your email list and offering them a discount when they buy clothes from your clothing line.

Besides that, you can send your customers special offers through email at certain times, like during the winter period when you want to clear old stock and replace them with newlines.

Steps to Scale Up in The Shortest Time Possible

The best way to scale your business high in the very shortest time possible is by strategizing and providing value to your customers.

The clothing line business is very competitive and so, you must be prepared to be different from others in the shortest time possible.

You can do this in the shortest time possible by following the steps below:

1. Offer home delivery and easy payment service

Not everyone will like to leave their homes to buy clothes and so, you need to provide the option for home delivery if you want to scale your business in a short time.

If a customer needs some clothes, they should be able to place their orders via phone call or leave their orders on your website and their order will be executed in the very shortest possible time.

This will enhance the scaling up of your clothing line business, gaining the trust of the customers, and increasing their loyalty and dependability on your business.

There is still another way of scaling your business up in a short time, that is to offer an easy payment service like a mobile POS system.

For customers who have little or no cash, they will be able to make use of their debit cards to effect payment for their purchased clothes.

2. Change or add more lines to your clothing line once a while

Some customers may get tired of buying similar clothes every single time and they may need a change. Be fashionable, be creative, productive, and bring more lines to the market place.

So, instead of customers having to search for another clothing line, they can easily come back to you knowing quite well that you have changed or added new lines. This is the more reason why you should keep updating them when you have newlines.

Your satisfied customers will become your advocate and even go as far as telling their friends and family members of your remarkable service; with all these, your business will expand in no distant future.

3. Grow your online presence

It is good to have an online presence but even better still, to grow it so that you can reach as many people as possible.

So getting to reach a lot of people will put you on your way to a long-term success since you are likely to be receiving new customers every day.

4. Provide your customers with something different from what others are offering

Your clothing line business should not only be about clothes that customers pay for. As a flourishing clothing line business owner, you should contemplate on something outside the box to make your customers happy.

For instance, you can partner with a company making face-cap to offer your customers a free face-cap to those who buy clothes from your store.

This will send a positive signal to your customers and they will also cherish the need to come back again and invite their friends as well.

5. Build an amazing brand

Many people get influenced by what they see and if you have a unique brand you will surely bring customers to your clothing line store.

Different ways to create an astonishing brand include creating an amazing logo, having an eye-catching name, and even hiring smart members of staff.

Mistakes to avoid

The clothing line business is indeed a lucrative one, especially if it is run in an area where fashionable people live who change clothes all the time.

Long time ago, the clothing line business has continued to grow around the world, serving people, fashionable and not-so fashionable people who change wardrobe all the time.

While the clothing business is a business formed to make money, there are some shortcomings and mistakes that can drag your business to the mud.

Here, we have put together some mistakes to avoid while operating your clothing line business:

1. Not setting your territory well

Customers are the backbone of a successful clothing line business. This is why every clothing line owner should set up his business in an area densely populated with potential customers.

Meanwhile, with a very good market survey and a precise marketing plan, you will go a long way in recognizing the area potential customers are found, their homes, and the workplaces.

Colleges, campuses, shopping malls, high streets and the internet are other areas you can explore when setting up your clothing line business.

2. Not going for original designs

In as much as you may be planning to save money, going for only private label, many people who are well to do may prefer original designers' label and are ready to pay. And failing to provide what they are willing and ready to buy will cause you to lose their patronage for good. So your market survey must be thorough to discover from the outset who your potential customers are and what is right for them.

3. Not welcoming or appreciating your customers

Top-class customer service should always be part of your administrative set up since you are in the fashion industry. Different classes of people visit your business site – online and your physical store. Have a friendly interactive website that will serve the potential customers in a friendly way and a physical store that will welcome them in the most dignified way. Asides from providing quality clothes, customers are also watchful of how they are being treated.

If you fail to appreciate or welcome customers particularly those that are highly valued, you may begin to lose them one after the other. On the flip side, if they are well appreciated and they know they are accorded the welcoming they deserve, they will continue to flood your clothing line store and even become your advocates.

4. Having a dirty and filthy environment.

Keeping the surrounding of your clothing line clean is crucial for a successful business. Your customers will not like to make a repeat purchase if the surrounding of the clothing store is filthy and unkempt

5.   Not having a social media presence

The world is now a global village and there is every need to make an online presence of your clothing business.

Social media is the media of the moment for spreading the news of everything happening around us all over the world, and to draw potential customers you must be connected to the internet. So for a start, you can have a Facebook page, Instagram handle, Twitter, and a website. You are going to have various designs of the designer's label and other private labels. On some occasions, you can post the activities of a fashion show, exhibition or a trade show on your site. You can write engaging content on your Instagram handles and Facebook pages too.

If people are pleased with what they see, they will likely visit your clothing line store for shopping.

Laws/Rules to Abide by to Avoid Legal Complications

Before launching your clothing line business, you must get the compulsory licenses and permits.

It may be difficult to give all the details of the licenses and permits because each country or state has its laws which may be different from each other.

But there are still some general licenses and permits which you are expected to get to avoid any legal complications.

The rules and regulations relating to the clothing line business to stay away from any legal complications are simply the licenses and permits which you have already.

It is usual for your local health department to issue you with these licenses and information that will guide you to carry on your business and be on the right side of the law.

The following are some of the rules and regulations every clothing line business owner is expected to be aware of to avoid any legal complications:

1. Apply to register your business as a sole proprietor or limited liability company and obtain a certificate of registration. For states such as California and NY, no registration is required; however, if you will be doing business under an assumed name, you will have to register with the county or state

2. Obtain the Federal and State Employer Identification Number. This is required if you are going to hire people to work for you.

3. Apply and obtain a permit to enable you to sell clothes and collect tax for the government. You will need a "Seller's Permit" and a "Certificate of

Authority" since apparels are taxable goods, so to run a clothing brand, you will need a license to sell clothes.

4. Apply and obtain a Garment/Apparel registration certificate to enable you to carry on business in the clothing industry. You need this certificate since many states in the US demand that you register your business with the state government if you are into manufacturing. The process of manufacturing may include cutting fabric, sewing, assembling, pressing and other related processes. Since you are going to have your clothing line (brand) you will also need to register.

5. Fire Department Permit is required when you have a retail shop or space for manufacturing, you will need to apply to the fire department and meet their strict guidelines to protect the employees of the clothing

company. You will need other permits if you have your own retail space like occupational permit, alarm permit, building permit, worker's compensation insurance, etc.

6. On sign permits, many cities have a way of controlling the nature of the signs you have outside your business. These may include size, lighting, and location among other things. Moreover, your landlord must approve the signs in writing before you fix them.
7. You will need the following insurance to operate: health insurance, disability insurance, business overhead expense disability insurance

Cloth Sewing Guidelines to Assure the Safety of Your Workers and Customers

If you will be working with sewing machines, you must understand its use as well as learn about the safety rules that apply to its use. The safety rules have been outlined to help you take good care of yourself when using the sewing machine.

Meanwhile, here are some safety guidelines that will assure the safety of your workers and customers:

1. Learn to keep the Distance

When feeding the needle with fabric as you are using the sewing machine, to be on the safe side, keep your finger at a safe distance. The distance may not be less than an inch away from the needle all the time.

Though sometimes you may have to guide your fabric to sew the path you would like to sew; even in that circumstances, you can obtain tools you can use to guide the fabric that doesn't put your finger in danger from the local craft store.

2. Keep Your Hair Out of the Way

You can't be that careless to allow your long hair to get close to the needle let alone getting caught up in the workings of your sewing machine. So if you have a long hair, use a hair tie or similar object to pull it back while working on the sewing machine

3. Concentrate

If you mount on the sewing machine working, to be safe, you must focus on the work you have on the sewing machine, if you want to stay safe. If you lose concentration, either you dose off or reaching for your phone, it is easy for an accident to take place by way of a simple slip of the hand.

4. Make Sure Your Pins and Needles Are Intact

As you are setting up your sewing machine to start work, be sure all pins and needles that will be used to work are undamaged in any way. This is because the damaged or broken needle can potentially damage your machine, the fabric or it can become a weapon that can injure you.

5. Never you Sew Over Pins

As we talk about damaged pins, never you attempt to sew on pins since potentially it can damage your machine or fabric or both. A broken needle when sewn can spin and fly at you. So do take pins out of your fabric as you are about to begin to sew.

6. Use the Right Machine

Using the right machine to sew cannot be overemphasized. If you are going to sew a particularly strong or thick fabric such as jeans, by all means, use a fitting sewing machine. If available, use an industrial sewing machine instead of the standard household machine. If you don't adhere to this, you risk damaging your machine.

7. Be Mindful of Electricity

As you use your sewing machine, you also make use of electricity to work. So you must be careful and use electricity in the right way. You can maintain safety if you take the necessary steps such as avoiding overloading outfits and not using damaged cables. When you notice something smells, the machine is shocking or there is the smoke of any kind, be quick to unplug and find out where the problem is.

8. Hear Your Machine

If at any time as you sew, you hear any rattling or grinding, for instance, you should sense that your machine has developed a problem and has to be checked out. Don't sew with a crack machine because if you do, the danger you face may be beyond your machine but may involve the problem of electricity.

10. Turn your machine Off When Not in Use

Always disconnect your sewing machine when out of commission. If your machine is plugged on when not in use, you risk causing an avoidable accident when someone who is not familiar with the dynamics accidentally pulls one of the machine handles.

How to Use Technology to Boost the Business

The world is rapidly turning into a global sphere of influence with technology taking the centre stage in this era.

As you have with other businesses, your clothing line needs to be technology-driven if it is to compete in this modern competitive world.

Here are some of the technologies you can adopt to boost your clothing line business; production and marketing of your wares.

1. Inter-business applications

Building applications for customers make sense. On the other hand, the clothing line can also benefit by making use of inter-business applications that aids in the running of the business.

For instance, there is an inter-business app that helps you in monitoring your fabric and the best temperature for it.

Besides, there are also some applications like the business app mint that helps clothing line business owners to track their business finances.

With the business app mint, clothing line owners use the software to track their expenses, follow their purchases, pay bills automatically, and to know their daily profit.

2.   Mobile POS System

This is the vital technology that helps people who are on the go without cash. It is also beneficial for the clothing line business because it enables them to receive money. What is required of the customer is to have the debit card and the PIN handy.

The swiftness of a mobile POS system further hastens transactions, especially when several people are waiting to be served.

Some of the advantages of using a mobile POS system include processing transactions online, tracking sales, and carrying out fast transactions.

Artificial intelligence (AI)

In the current market competition, clothing lines and brands have been using AI to improve customers' shopping experience, get data analyzed, generate high sales, predict trends and offer inventory-related control, and so on.

On its part, TRUEFIT uses an online fit engine to get users to find a good fit with brands and styles on the market.

STYUMIA in its way generates information from images, user behavior data, textual descriptions from social media to assist clothing line and fashion designers to make brand decisions about where their brands are going.

Internet of Things (IOT)

The increasing expansion of technology has positively affected businesses in many ways. The Internet of Things (IoT) permits data sharing, security, inventory management, and increased efficiency and productivity.

Many businesses give kudos to IOT in improving their customer experience.

Another good example of the internet of things being integrated in apparel is LOOMIA. This is made possible by the San Francisco-based textile company that creates soft flexible circuits that can be implanted into textiles and can be used for sensing or data-tracking applications, heating, lighting, etc.

Rapid Data Analysis for Quick Adaptation

This is internet based; it's a new software tools currently in the market, available to brands and factories which can receive real-time feedback and alerts from companies concerning defects or damaged goods. This allows making amends on time thereby saving money, eliminating waste, and deliver the right products promptly.

Mobile Commerce

The use of smartphones for shopping online is becoming easier by the day. This is made possible with the use of digital wallet options like Apple and Android Pay. Work is increasingly going on with the new technologies like fingerprint and facial recognition, in the hope that they will replace the current methods of payment for retail purchases.

Other Books by the Same Author

- How to Start a Photography Business: A Beginner's Guide to A Successful Career as A Photographer
- How to Invest in Real Estate (For Beginners): Make Your First $100,000 Using This Powerful Real Estate Business Model
- How to Start A Drop Shipping Business: Make Your First $1,000 Using This Powerful Drop Shipping Business Model
- How to Start a Cleaning Business: Make Your First $100,000 Using This Powerful Commercial Cleaning Business Model
- How to Start a Life Coaching Business: Foolproof Guide for

Establishing a Successful Life-Coaching Career

Printed in Great Britain
by Amazon